Leisure Arts 6
Painting
Flowers
in Watercolour
Sarah Jane Coleridge

SEARCH PRESS
Wellwood North Farm Road Tunbridge Wells

Introduction

I enjoy painting flowers because it is exciting to create their colour, tone and form on paper and to try to recapture the characteristics of each part of a growing plant. You need skill to paint subtle shades of pink, pale lemon yellows, quiet blues and vibrant reds. With experience, it is possible to mix colours so that the shades are neither too bright nor too pale. You also need patience and application to learn to handle paint successfully. Practice and learn from your mistakes as this will develop your style and ability more than anything else.

I am often disappointed with the result of some paintings, as so many things can go wrong; bad composition, wrong colour or tone balance, or lack of clarity. In this book, I have outlined the most important points to remember when painting flowers: obtaining an effect of light, arranging flowers, positioning flowers, drawing, colour, working in detail and creating an overall balance.

Paint as many different types of flower as you can. If you keep struggling with a bunch of roses, for instance, your enthusiasm will evaporate quickly. A sunflower may look different in structure to a daffodil, but basically the same principles of colour and texture apply. The paintings in this book may contain plants with which you are not familiar. I hope you can overlook this and understand the essential techniques: you can then apply these to any flowers. With observation and practice, you will have endless enjoyment from painting flowers.

A simple lateral arrangement of a pansy and a rock rose. Small flowers make as strong an impact as large ones if treated with care.

Materials

Always buy good quality materials. Here are a few tips that I find useful when painting flowers.

Paper

Watercolour paper varies in size, thickness and surface. If you are a beginner, examine the papers carefully to see how they vary. When looking at watercolour paintings, note the paper used and how it affects the brushstrokes and the way the paint lies on the paper surface. You can buy paper in single sheets, but if you have nowhere to store it, buy a pad. I use mostly 356 × 254mm/14 × 10 in. Bockingford 295 gsm/140 lb. paper. This is quite thick and has a reasonably rough surface, so that when water is applied the paper does not rumple as ordinary sketching paper does. Many watercolourists use paper that needs stretching so that it does not rumple after the application of a wide flat wash. When painting flowers, I do not use much water on the paper and so find that a spiral bound block of watercolour paper is quite suitable and does not need stretching.

There are some beautiful hand-made papers that are a delight to paint on, but they are expensive.

Take care not to crease watercolour paper and damage the surface. Some papers have a right and wrong side. Make sure you use the right one.

Paints

I use artist quality paints which have a more oily texture than student paints which sometimes dry out after a time. Pans of colour are more difficult to keep clean which is an important consideration for this style of work. Buy tubes of paint individually and begin with a few colours. I use the following colours: lemon yellow, cadmium yellow, yellow ochre, raw umber, cadmium red, alizarin crimson, rose doré, sap green, cobalt blue, cerulean blue, burnt sienna and burnt umber.

Drawing

An HB pencil is ideal for lightly drawing in the flowers before beginning to paint. A good quality rubber is useful for erasing mistakes.

Brushes

As most of the brushwork for this style of painting is very fine, it is necessary to have only a few brushes. I use sable brushes nos. 2, 1, 0 and 00. Squirrel hair brushes are cheaper but not as pleasant to use as sable.

Small flowers make excellent fillers in arrangements. Here gypsophila and viscaria have been painted with detail that does justice to their delicacy.

I thoroughly enjoyed painting this honeysuckle as it had such an interesting shape. Offset two large petunias with a collection of smaller flowers and leaves. Paint the honeysuckle stamens carefully to add the finishing touch. The two central leaves were very difficult to place behind the honeysuckle because they threatened to disrupt the composition.

page 5
An enlarged section of the honeysuckle showing brushwork detail over the fine pencil line work.

Working method

It is easier to paint flowers indoors as the arrangement remains still and you are not distracted by inclement weather. As I do not have a studio, I usually work in a bedroom and sit at a window sill with the flowers in a vase in front of me. I use the wide window ledge for my art materials.

After setting out paper and paints, pick a small bunch of flowers. If you do not have a garden, buy flowers from a market stall, as they are usually more expensive at a garden shop. I try to incorporate a plan of certain colours into a picture, for example, yellow roses with blue surrounding flowers, or a bright red and yellow colour scheme as in the poppy painting on page 17. Collect flowers with a colour scheme in mind rather than picking anything you can find. Don't pick more than you really need, as flowers do not look fresh for long after being indoors. Arrange the flowers in a vase in front of where you work and decide which flower to paint first.

Begin by lightly drawing a careful outline of the first flower so that it can be rubbed out later on. There are some flowers lightly drawn in pencil on page 7. Be particular when drawing a flower and study the shape carefully. An inaccurate drawing will cause much dissatisfaction with the finished painting. It is not easy at first, but with a little practice, you will quickly improve. Keep all your early drawings, as it is constructive and encouraging to glance back at your first pictures and discover that you are gradually improving!

Use a no. 1 watercolour brush to apply a little water on to the paper where the flower is drawn. Do not make the paper too wet or let the water run over the pencil edge; the paper must be moist enough to absorb the first wash of paint quite easily, without it appearing scratched or rubbed on to the paper. Examples showing how to apply paint to paper are on page 8. In example 1 the brush and paper were too dry and the paint has not sunk in but has had to be worked on to the paper, producing a dry effect. Experiment on a spare sheet of watercolour paper and discover for yourself how much water you need to put on the brush and paper, before tackling the first flower. At first the technique is tricky to grasp, but it will soon develop.

To paint the petunia in example 4, mix together a little alizarin crimson and rose doré. Make sure the paper is still moist and apply a light wash of pale pink. Keep this first wash light in colour, or the contrast between the light and dark colours of the finished flower will be spoiled and the flower will appear rather heavy and flat and lose its delicate translucent effect. When you have painted the first wash, mix a darker shade of the pink, add a little cobalt blue and apply this colour where a deeper shade of pink is needed. At this stage, the first wash of paint must be damp, or the second wash will not be absorbed effectively, and instead of the washes merging together, the second wash will appear rather hard and dry leaving a noticeable line.

Sometimes if the paper is too wet, the paint dries unevenly and leaves a thin darkish line of colour around the flower. When this happens, take a damp brush, carefully lift out the dark line, and wipe the brush on a rag.

At this point, there are two shades of pink on the flower. Now mix an even darker shade of the original pink and paint in the very dark areas of the flower, for instance.The flower centre and where one petal overlaps another. Add the fine little veins which are often visible in the petals, drawing them in carefully with a fine brush. Finally, lightly rub out the pencil outline.

Remember to try and paint what you see, and give enough detail and work to a flower so that it looks reasonably life-like. Do not overwork the details or the flower will become too botanical in appearance.

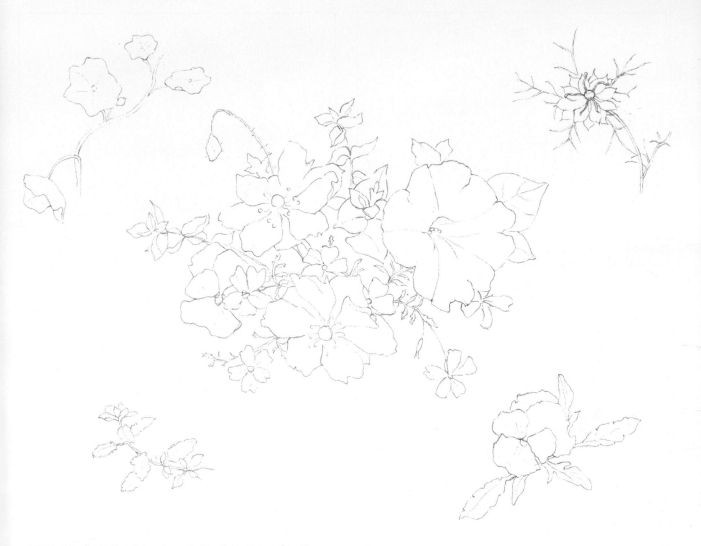

I have included quite a lot of detail in these drawings as it is important to establish the characteristics of each flower. Do not draw too hard when doing this or the thin washes of paint will come off when the outline is erased after painting.

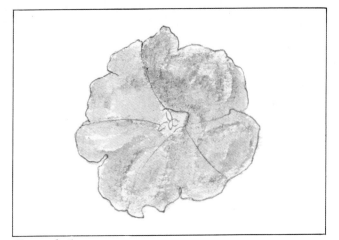

Example 1 – wrong

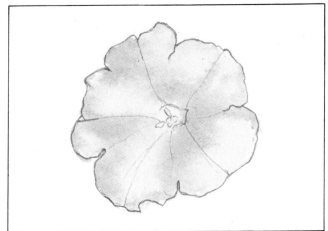

Example 2 – right

Example 3 – wrong

Example 4 – right

Example 1 – wrong

The paper was too dry when the petals were painted and so produced ugly patches giving a scratched appearance. Keep the paper moist enough to float the paint evenly and try to put the paint on in one go; a double-layered wash loses luminosity.

Example 2 – right

A good moist background has encouraged the paint to disperse softly.

Example 3 – wrong

The dark shadows added after the first wash were too hard and strong causing the whole flower to look messy and unrealistic.

Example 4 – right

Areas of soft dark shadow were dabbed on while the first wash was still wet which gives a delicate effect. If the first wash has dried, put blobs of water on the petals and let them disperse, but take care not to leave hard thin edges.

This painting looks far more difficult than it is. I began with the large blooms and added in smaller flowers one by one until the right balance was achieved. The greatest challenge was to paint the white rose and orange-centered dimorphothecas. The large white rose has a very soft wash across its petals and is painted mainly in grey, with a little lemon yellow at the base of some of the petals. Mix some burnt umber with the grey and paint the veins of the petals on to a dry background. The other two daisy-like flowers have a very pale orange wash across the petals – they are far from being just white paper. I used Naples yellow on the three large yellow flowers as it is more opaque than lemon or cadmium yellow.

Leaves

Leaves are an integral part of painting flowers. Used carefully in an arrangement, they provide balance in colour and shape and offset flowers to great effect. Leaf colours, shapes and textures are extremely varied; study them in the paintings in this book and notice how many of the paintings would be very dull without them.

A rose leaf is an easy leaf to paint. It has an attractive shape and I often include it in a painting where there is a problem with composition. When painting a rose leaf, notice the reddish-brown colouring at the base of the leaf and at the jagged edge of the point. Put in the fine veins as a few small details like this give credibility to a painting. Experiment by painting some unusual-shaped leaves. These are good subjects if you can find them. Nasturtium has a round shaped leaf with effective markings, but quite difficult to paint. Polyanthus has a cumbersome leaf that looks excellent if you are able to capture the rough texture and the fresh bright green colouring. Daffodil is a beautiful blue-green colour but is awkward and long. To counteract this, I sometimes place this leaf behind a flower thereby suggesting a large leaf without actually showing it.

Do not use too many leaves in one painting or the abundance of green will kill the sparkle in the work. Use variegated leaves such as those of ivy or periwinkle to give relief from too much green.

Light

Light gives sparkle and a certain life to a flower painting. Without light, a flower looks flat and dull. Study the single rose and leaves on page 13 and notice the effect of the pale undercoat contrasting with the different shades of green on the leaves. If dark green had been painted all over the leaf, the effect of light would disappear leaving a flat plane. Study the flower you are

Example 1 – wrong

painting and see the areas where light falls on the petals. Leave these parts very light and the painting will have more impact.

I never use white paint when using white watercolour paper. To achieve a light effect, think ahead and plan which areas need to be left white before putting any paint on the paper. If you do use white paint for the highlights, you will lose some of the translucence that is so important in watercolour painting.

Example 1 – wrong

These leaves are flat and have no life as the basic wash is not graduated.

Example 2 – right

The same leaves are more varied here due to the way the wash was applied. Leave areas of white and incorporate hard and soft lines in the leaf colours as well as in the veins.

A single rose: demonstration

Stage 1

Draw in the outline of the rose, taking care to do it lightly so that it is easy to erase.

Stage 2

Wet the flower head and put in a very pale alizarin crimson wash. Work on no more than two petals at a time and use rose doré for the darker petals but leave

Example 2 – right

plenty of white on the outer edges. Put pale lemon yellow wash over the leaves, using a very small amount of paint.

Stage 3

Put a second wash over the base of the petals, using cadmium red for variety. Make sure the leaves are still slightly moist and then add sap green and cobalt blue mixed in varying proportions for the darker areas and leave areas of pale yellow to show light. A subtle variation in colour is already apparent on the leaves.

Stage 4

Strengthen the colour of the petals by adding cobalt blue to alizarin crimson. When there is enough colour on the leaves and petals, paint the veins with a mixture of cobalt blue, sap green and burnt umber. On no account use black to do this. Do the veining when parts of each leaf and petal are still moist so that a broken line is produced with hard and soft edges.

Stage 5

There is very little difference in these last two stages. If all the work on this painting is successful so far, then all that remains to be done is to bring out the softness of the rose. It looks a little harsh in stage 4, so soften some of the edges of the veins on the leaves and petals. Be extremely cautious when doing this as too much blending will result in loss of character.

Stage 1

Stage 2

Stage 3

Stage 4

Stage 5 — the finished painting

Arranging flowers

There are two ways of working, either arrange the flowers into an attractive group before painting, or arrange them as you paint on the paper. I use the second method and without any preconceived arrangement in mind, I build up the picture flower by flower as I paint. If you are familiar with flowers, then this is a successful method and intuition will prevent mistakes. Disasters do happen, but it is still possible to save a painting.

I begin by painting the main flower and usually two or three others. I then add smaller flowers and leaves to complement the main flowers. The painting of poppies on the back cover was produced in this way. I painted the poppies and then introduced other interesting flowers and foliage. Note the effectiveness of the small poppy buds: without these and the dangling daisies, the painting would look too solid. On page 15 the drawing of a poppy arrangement without any small flowers illustrates the point perfectly.

The main points to remember when arranging flowers are to compare and contrast colours, shapes and textures. This will produce interesting paintings and ensure against using the same design.

Poppies: demonstration

Stage 1

After drawing in the outline of the poppies, begin work on one flower head and wet some of the petals. Let the water soak into the paper and then dab paint on with a no. 1 sable brush but control the diffusion carefully. The colours used are lemon yellow and cadmium red. If you put on too much paint, lift out excess colour with a clean moist brush.

Stage 2

Work just on the two poppy heads until they are complete. While the paper is still moist, blend in subtle shades of red made from different combinations of cadmium red, lemon yellow, cobalt blue and burnt umber. Paint a stigma in the centre of each flower with dark cobalt blue. Add the thin dark lines on the petals with a no. 0 sable brush. Paint into both dry and wet paper to achieve a broken line. Put in the stamens around the stigma then lay a thin lemon yellow wash over the poppy bud.

Stage 3

Add sap green to the poppy bud while it is still wet. Let it dry and flick fine hairs on to the stem with a no. 00 sable brush.

Stage 4

Put the first pale lemon yellow wash over the nemesia. Use the same procedure to do this as for the two finished poppy heads. Painting flowers in this style is

not difficult if you follow these simple techniques, concentrate and above all consider each brushstroke before applying paint to paper.

This is an example of how an arrangement of large shapes lacks interest and looks dreamy. Add small flowers and other details and this will give it freshness.

Stage 5 (*shown on back cover*)

There is a great deal of difference between the last two stages. I am not particularly happy with the finished painting, as all the round shapes make the arrangement too intense but it is saved to a certain extent by the spiky poppy leaves and straggly buds. I had great difficulty in positioning the dark yellow nasturtium as its colour was similar in weight to the poppies. The white flower in the centre of the picture complements the poppies well and provides space between the strong red shapes. The drooping poppy on the extreme right is the most successful as its pose is so striking. The tiny blue flowers contrast well against so much red.

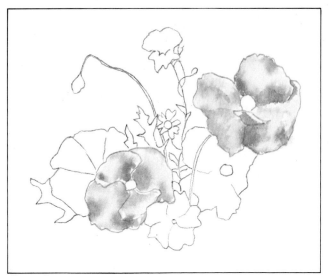

Stage 1

Stage 2

Stage 3

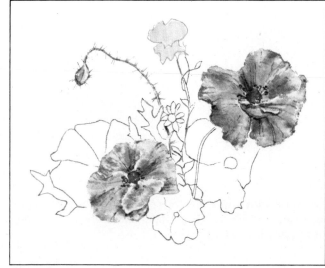

Stage 4

page 17
This enlargement shows the fine detail created by hard and soft edges and tonal variations achieved by overlaying washes.

Detail of the finished painting shown on the back cover.

Positioning flowers

The positioning of a flower is very important. Sometimes a flower appears more attractive if the head is tilted at an angle instead of face-on. Experiment with your flowers and you will understand what I mean. For example, let a daffodil dangle its head over the edge of a vase, or lay it on a book and let the flower head fall to one side. If it is necessary to raise the head slightly, simply support it with a paint tube.

Move the flower into different positions to find its most appealing angle and study the different ways in which the light falls on the petals. Even the back view of a flower can look effective in a picture.

A few daffodils with their heads face-on are on page 21. Compare these with those on page 32 in which two of the daffodils on the left are tilted at different angles. These daffodils appear more realistic and graceful than the others.

Colour

When painting flowers in watercolour I attempt to capture the colour of the real flower as accurately as possible. This is not always easy, but as you increase your skill with paint you will have a better chance of achieving the right colour. Do not mix too many colours together or the colour you produce may appear rather muddy. A good rule is to mix together no more than three colours. In the painting on page 21, I aimed to produce a bright colourful picture but that did not appear brash or gaudy. It is easy to use too much colour and ruin a painting, so I try to have two or three bright patches of colour and then use more moderate colouring in the rest of the picture. In the demonstration on page 20, I found the white daffodils with the yellow-orange centres much easier to paint then the plain yellow daffodils. The contrast of the silvery pale petals against the brilliant yellow-orange centre is quite striking. A plain golden daffodil, despite its glorious yellow, can look dull and heavy if you make the dark shadows on the flower too strong.

The polyanthus flower is exciting to paint and these flowers add a great deal of life to a picture as they look so rich and vibrant. Despite this, I avoid the brightest colours as I am wary of sacrificing subtlety for brightness. It is important not to overfill a picture with flowers and leaves. The painting on page 21 was becoming coarse and weighty with too many daffodils and polyanthus leaves. To balance the picture, I included a few small delicate flowers which solved the problem.

A simple but carefully painted group containing nigella, clary, lobelia and gypsophila.

Daffodils: demonstration

Stage 1

Make a simple drawing of the central flower and some of the smaller details. Wash pale lemon yellow over the daffodil and then lay a second variegated wash of cadmium yellow over the trumpet.

Stage 2

Make up a grey from sap green and cobalt blue and lay in areas of shadow on the petals, the trumpet and in the centre. When the petals are almost dry, paint in lines to give them form and shape. Lay a lemon yellow wash over the polyanthus.

Stage 3

Paint the polyanthus petals with rose doré and alizarin crimson and try to obtain a soft effect of broken colour. Use cadmium yellow for the centre and when dry, paint in lines which give them character. Lay a pale lemon wash over the large leaf in the foreground.

Stage 4

Work up the colour in the leaf by adding tiny blobs of cobalt blue and sap green on to the wet paper. Watch the diffusion of this colour carefully and ensure that

A careful drawing of two petunias. Practice drawing flowers at every opportunity.

Stage 1

Stage 2

Stage 3

Stage 4

large areas of white remain visible. When the paper is almost dry use the same technique as for the petals, and paint in fine lines to create a realistic texture.

Stage 5

This painting was done by repeating the technique described in stages 1 – 4. Painting flowers in this style is not difficult. There are no secret methods or complex tricks.

I think the overall effect of this painting is clumsy as

Stage 5 — the finished painting

nearly all the daffodils are face-on and the green leaf on the right is too large and dark. Again the picture is rescued by the small flowers. The trumpet of the daffodil on the top left is badly drawn, but the flower in the centre is more successful because the lines that come up and out of the trumpet give it depth.

Flower shapes

Consider the shape of every flower carefully as some types such as aster, chrysanthemum and marigold are much more difficult to draw than others. Though these are lovely flowers, their shape is round and heavy, which makes them tricky to paint successfully. The poppy also has a round and heavy shape, but as it is a very light and flimsy flower, it is easier to paint in watercolour.

Flowers with shapes that are challenging to draw are nasturtiums, fuschias, snap dragons, foxgloves with their lovely bell-shaped heads and majestic gladiolae which bloom in such delightful salmon pink and pale orange colours.

It is not always necessary to draw a complete flower. In the painting on page 25, I placed a deep red poppy behind the central pink and white one, so that the red one was just hinted at, and helped to show up the paler, more delicate poppy. Draw and paint in part of a flower when you have an awkward space in the arrangement. This is more interesting than trying to squeeze in a complete flower.

Aubretia, rock rose and primrose are three small flowers that make excellent subjects for practicing controlled use of colour. Note that the leaves have a stronger colour than the flowers.

Small details

It is important to take particular care in painting stems and buds. It is no good having a pretty flower head on a willowy, badly-drawn stem. Give a stem enough body so that it looks as if it can support the flower head. In the painting on page 25, observe the detail on the poppy flowers such as the little stamens in the centre of the flower. Look closely at the two poppy buds: these are covered in tiny little hairs, which help to make the poppy buds more life-like. Without these small hairs, the poppies look incomplete. I painted the poppies first and surrounded them with gypsophila (the little white flowers), clary (the small pink flowers) and viscaria (the blue-mauve flowers). If you have a garden, sow a few annual seeds as they are most useful in painting this type of picture.

To give a painting interest, put in small buds or half-opened flowers as well as full blooms. Take care over the buds or they will look like small blobs of paint. I find that if a painting turns out satisfactorily, it is partly because I have spent time observing and painting the small details of the flowers and leaves.

Shirley poppies: demonstration

Stage 1

Outline the centre poppy and some of the surrounding flowers in pencil. Moisten the poppy with a little water and introduce very pale washes of alizarin crimson taking care to keep the outside edges of the petals white. While the paper is still wet, dab lemon yellow in the centre of the flower and at the base of some of the petals making sure there are no hard lines.

Stage 2

Paint a second wash of alizarin crimson on the petals, mix grey from cobalt blue and sap green and apply it at the base of the centre petals to give depth. Use sap green to show the stigma and paint the stamens with dots of cadmium yellow and yellow ochre. Add a touch of cadmium red to the petals but keep the outer edges white so that they seem to sparkle.

Stage 3

Complete the centre poppy by adding veins in pale grey. Begin work on the other two poppies using cadmium red and plenty of water.

Stage 4

Add deeper shades of red and when dry mix cadmium red with cobalt blue and put in the lines and tiny areas of dark shadow.

Notice how the pink poppy is highlighted by the deeper, darker red flower behind it. I often use this composition as I know it works well.

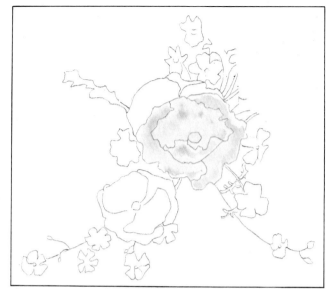

Stage 1

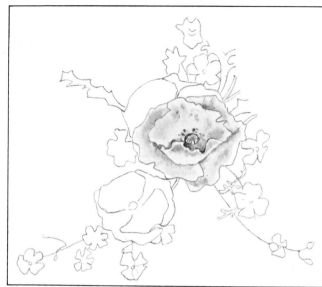

Stage 2

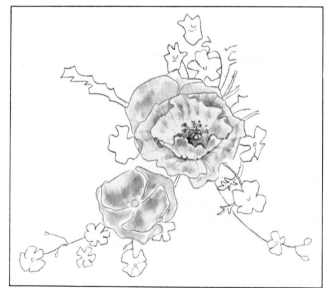

Stage 3

Stage 4

Stage 5

How you arrange the composition of flowers is your own choice. There are few rules but it is easy to make mistakes when beginning. Try to maintain a balance of colour, form and shape. This does not necessarily mean it has to be symmetrical as visual contradiction often gives good results.

Although I have some reservations regarding the

Stage 5 — the finished painting

composition of this painting, it does have a pleasing
overall effect as there is plenty of light and sparkle
from the white edges of the shirley poppies.

Dark shadows
and deep colours

Painting the deep-coloured shadows or contrasting the light and dark parts of a flower presents particular problems in watercolour. Remember that it is only necessary to paint what you see, so if a dark shadow is visible, try to paint it exactly as you see it. Without these dark shadows, the flowers may seem pretty and attractive, but they are less realistic and have no depth. Dark shadows throw up the highlights to great effect. To help isolate light and dark areas, look at the flowers through half closed eyes for a moment and the tonal differences may then seem more obvious.

In the painting on page 29, I worked on the narcissi first. These flowers had very delicate pale lemon coloured petals and the two central flowers had silvery white ones. To portray these fragile flowers accurately, I had to carefully paint in greenish-grey shadows to emphasize the petals. The narcissi also had bluish-green stems with hints of very dark green which helped to contrast with the pale delicate petals. The rich yellow colour in the centre of the narcissi also enhanced the petals.

The small dark leaves and flowers balance well with the large, light, airy petunia.

Having completed the narcissi, I worked on the primroses and alyssum, two more delicate spring flowers. When these were finished, I noticed that although these soft yellow flowers looked very pretty, they needed a strong-coloured flower or leaf to give depth to the painting and to bring out the beauty of the pale flowers, so I incorporated several pansies into the painting and found that the mauve and alizarin crimson colour of these flowers achieved this perfectly. A few leaves also provided a contrast to the flowers. I could have added more richly-coloured flowers, but I wanted a very delicate spring picture of mostly lemon yellow flowers, offset by a few deeper coloured ones rather than have an arrangement of many different coloured spring flowers.

Narcissi: demonstration

Stage 1

Draw the flower in the centre of the composition. Follow the same procedure described in the other demonstrations. Lay a pale lemon yellow wash over the outer petals and while still moist, paint in the grey mixed from sap green and cobalt blue. Notice that a hard edge is apparent where the paper has dried on the lowest petal. Use sap green for the stem.

Stage 2

Add more grey to the base of the petals and some bright dashes of cadmium yellow to the centre. Give the stem more body by working in a few brushstrokes of darker green and add some burnt umber to the shoot on the left. Erase the pencil line around the edge of the petals and notice how much softer the flower seems. Paint fine grey lines on the petals and then start the same sequence for the next bloom.

A star-shaped arrangement around a pansy.

Detail 1

The large pale blooms contrast well with the small dark leaves and purple flowers. Place the dark flowers behind the lighter ones to create depth and ensure balance. Study the brushwork in this detail and try to determine which strokes were made into wet paper. This analysis shows how easy this style of watercolour painting is.

Detail 2

This section of the painting looks overbearing when shown out of context. The blooms jostle for position and there is little light and air in the picture in comparison to the finished painting in stage 3. This is a good example of the importance of the use of space to create a light effect.

Stage 3

I struggled with this painting as I was sure it was going to turn out looking too busy. On reflection it works quite well. Although there is a lot happening, the composition is not too tight. The two dark pansies throw out the soft yellows and give weight to a painting that does not have much strong, rich colour.

Stage 1

Stage 2

Detail 1

Detail 2

Stage 3 – the finished painting

Mounting and framing

Nothing ruins a good painting more than bad mounting or framing. If you have worked hard and produced a fine piece of work, it is worth going to the trouble and expense of presenting it to its best advantage. If you know nothing about mounting or framing find someone who can do it for you.

Mounting is easier than framing and is quite simple to learn. Good mounting card is available from most art shops and is manufactured in different thicknesses as well as a wide range of colours. Choose a colour that is harmonious to the painting and does not over-power it. Spend time calculating how much white paper is necessary around the flowers. If the mount is too close to the flowers they will look squashed and insignificant. If there is too much white, the mount and frame will look more important than the painting itself. A bevelled edge is essential on the inside of the mount and it is easy to do this after practicing on an old sheet of card with a steel rule and a knife with a retractable

blade. Apply a lot of pressure to obtain a good clean cut and always keep your fingers behind the cutting blade whenever possible. A subtle wash line around the inside edge of the mount will enhance your work even more if used with discretion and sensitivity.

A useful method of judging the ideal width of a mount is to cut two large L-shaped pieces of card and position them at opposite sides of a painting. Move them in and out until you obtain the desired effect. Keep them in your studio for regular use and a small selection of mounts that you can lay over a newly-finished painting to decide on shape and colour.

Of all subjects, portraits and flowers are best suited to round or oval mounts. The latter are fairly easy to obtain from good craft or art shops. It is very difficult to cut an oval mount by hand unless you practice a great deal. It is extremely enjoyable to paint flowers in miniature. Small well executed paintings have as much impact as some larger works.

Seasonal flowers

When you are painting flowers, it is better to try to keep to their appropriate seasons If you paint throughout the winter, you will notice the benefit of this practice when the flowers come out again in Spring.

Throughout the year, take care to look for wild flowers in the hedges and fields. These wild specimens can look delightful with a few grasses and other foliage. In general, wild flowers do not have the brightness of colour that cultivated plants have, but their colours, shapes and textures are more subtle and look very striking when they are painted with observation, patience and consideration.

ACKNOWLEDGMENTS

First published in Great Britain 1980
Search Press Limited,
Wellwood, North Farm Road,
Tunbridge Wells, Kent TN2 3DR.

12th impression 1994

Text, drawings and painting by Sarah Jane Coleridge.

Text, illustrations, arrangement and typography copyright © Search Press Limited 1981.

I should like to thank Mrs Penelope Lebus for letting me paint roses from her garden.

UK ISBN 0 85532 405 8

Front and back views of shirley poppies.

Distributors to the art trade:

UK
Winsor & Newton,
Whitefriars Avenue, Wealdstone,
Harrow, Middlesex HA3 5RH

USA
ColArt Americas Inc.,
11 Constitution Avenue, P. O. Box 1396, Piscataway, NJ 08855-1396

Arthur Schwartz & Co.,
234 Meads Mountain Road, Woodstock, NY 12498

Canada
Anthes Universal Limited,
341 Heart Lake Road South, Brampton, Ontario L6W 3K8

Australia
Max A. Harrell
P. O. Box 92, Burnley, Victoria 3121

Jasco Pty, Limited
937-941 Victoria Road, West Ryde, N.S.W. 2114

New Zealand
Caldwell Wholesale Limited,
Wellington and Auckland

South Africa
Ashley & Radmore (Pty) Limited,
P. O. Box 2794, Johannesburg 2000

Trade Winds Press (Pty) Limited,
P. O. Box 20194, Durban North 4016

Made and printed in Spain by Artes Graphicas Elkar, S. Coop.
Autonomía, 71 - 48012-Bilbao - Spain.

This spring flower arrangement includes daffodils, chinadoxia, polyanthus, primrose, cowslip and a cherry branch. I wanted a predominantly yellow painting and so I used cadmium and lemon yellow for most of the flowers. The large primrose in the foreground on the left has a pale lemon wash over the petals and a little cadmium yellow added to the centre of the flower to give it depth. The orange centres of the two middle daffodils were made by adding a dash of cadmium red to cadmium yellow. Use of grey gives texture to the petals. The grey is a mixture of cobalt blue, sap green and a touch of burnt umber. I also painted some on to the wet petals over the basic yellow wash. Some of these petals have hard grey edges where the paper dried before the colour was applied. The other hard-edged grey lines on the petals were added later. Do not leave out the dark creases at the base of daffodil trumpets or they will look flat.

The upright daffodil in the centre and the one on the right face-on, are positioned at less interesting angles than the two on the left which turned out more successfully.